The magic swan and The sad princess

Hannie Truijens

Illustrated by Margaret Sherry

The magic swan page 2

The sad princess page 13

Nelson

The magic swan

Once upon a time there were three
brothers called Amos, Jake and
Benjamin.
They lived next to a big wood.
One day Amos said to Benjamin,
"Put some meat and wine into
my bag."
Then Amos went to the wood to cut
down a big tree.

Chop, chop, chop, went the axe.
Amos sat down to rest and eat.
A dwarf came and sat next to him.
"Will you give me some of your
meat and wine?" said the dwarf.

"No," said Amos.

"You'll be sorry," said the dwarf.

"Wait and see, you'll be sorry."

Amos went back to his chopping.

Chop, chop, chop, went the axe.

It fell and cut Amos on the arm.

Amos came home and went to bed.

His arm was very, very sore.

Jake had to go and cut down
the tree.

"Put some meat and wine into my
bag," he said to Benjamin.

Chop, chop, chop, went the axe.
Jake sat down to rest and eat.
The dwarf came to sit next to him.
"Will you give me some of your
meat and wine?" said the dwarf.

"No," said Jake.

"You'll be sorry," said the dwarf.

"Wait and see, you'll be sorry."

Jake went back to his chopping.

Chop, chop, chop, went the axe.

It fell and cut Jake on the leg.

Jake came home and went to bed.
His leg was very, very sore.
Benjamin had to go and cut down
the tree.
All that was left for him was
bread and water.

Chop, chop, chop, went the axe.
Benjamin sat down to rest and eat.
"Will you give me some of your
bread and water?" said the dwarf.
"Yes," said Benjamin, "here you are."

"You are very kind," said the dwarf.
"Here is a present for you.
It is a magic swan.
It will help you, wait and see."

Benjamin took the swan home.

"What a fine, fat swan," said Amos.

"It will be very good to eat,"
said Jake.

"No, no," said Benjamin.

"You can't eat my swan."

He took the swan and ran away.

Benjamin had no home, no bed and no food.

He looked at his swan.

"What am I going to do?" he said.

"The dwarf said that you could help me.

Can you help me now, please?"

Will the magic swan help Benjamin?

Read the next story and find out.

The sad princess

The sad princess looked out of
the castle.
She didn't smile.
She didn't laugh.
She was always sad.
"I don't know what to do with her,"
said the king.
"I wish we could make her laugh."

Benjamin walked to the castle
with his magic swan.
"I will ask them to help me,"
he said.
An old man saw the fine, fat swan
and tried to get it.

His hand stuck to the swan's tail.
"Help, help," cried the old man.
"I am stuck to this swan."
An old woman saw the old man
and came to help him.

Her hand stuck to the old man.

"Help, help," cried the old woman.

"I am stuck to this old man."

A big girl saw the old woman and
came to help her.

Her hand stuck to the old woman.
"Help, help," cried the big girl.
"I am stuck to this old woman."
A small boy saw the big girl and
came to help her.

His hand stuck to the big girl.
"Help, help," cried the small boy.
"I am stuck to this big girl."
A little black dog saw the
small boy and came to help him.

His teeth stuck to the small boy.
Benjamin went on walking.
The man, the woman, the girl,
the boy and the little black dog
had to go with him.
"Help, help," they cried.
"Grrr," said the little black dog.

The sad princess saw Benjamin,
the swan, the old man,
the old woman, the big girl,
the small boy and
the little black dog.
They made her laugh.
They made her laugh and laugh.

The king was very happy.
"You have made the princess laugh,"
he said to Benjamin.
"Would you and your swan like to
live in the castle with us?"

The swan let go of the old man,
the old woman, the big girl,
the small boy and
the little black dog.
The princess took Benjamin into
the castle.

Benjamin and the princess were
happy in the castle.
The magic swan was very happy in
the water.
And the king was very, very
happy.

Whenever the princess was sad
she looked at the magic swan.
Then she remembered the man,
the woman, the girl, the boy and
the little black dog.
And she laughed and laughed.